City Life, Farm Life

written by Wendy Graham

Engage Literacy is published in 2013 by Raintree.
Raintree is an imprint of Capstone Global Library Limited, a company incorporated in Engand and Wales having its registered office at 7 Pilgrim Street, London, EC4V 6LB – Registered company number: 6695582
www.raintreepublishers.co.uk

Originally published in Australia by Hinkler Education, a division of Hinkler Books Pty Ltd.
Text and illustration copyright © Hinkler Books Pty Ltd 2012

Written by Wendy Graham
Lead authors Jay Dale and Anne Giulieri
Edited by Gwenda Smyth
UK edition edited by Dan Nunn, Catherine Veitch and Sian Smith
Designed by Susannah Low, Butterflyrocket Design

City Life, Farm Life
ISBN: 978 1 406 26515 6
10 9 8 7 6 5 4 3 2

Printed and bound in China by Leo Paper Products Ltd

Acknowledgements
Cover images (top to bottom): © Leo Bruce Hempell | Dreamstime.com; iStockphoto.com/ © Ben Klaus; p4: © Leo Bruce Hempell | Dreamstime.com; p5 main: © Rivertracks | Dreamstime.com; p5 inset: iStockphoto.com/ © Vicki Reid; p6 top: iStockphoto.com/ © Yvan Dubé; p6 bottom: iStockphoto.com/ © Querbeet; p7: iStockphoto.com/ © Ben Klaus; p8 main: © Valentino Visentini | Dreamstime.com; p8 inset: Imagebroker.net/SuperStock; p9 top left: Two British Police Constables © Howard Sayer/Shutterstock; p9 top right: © Wavebreakmedia Ltd | Dreamstime.com; p9 bottom: iStockphoto.com/ © Deborah Cheramie; p10 top: © Kateleigh | Dreamstime.com; p10 middle: Juice Images/SuperStock; p10 bottom: iStockphoto.com/ © Susan H. Smith; p11 main: © Anthony Aneese Totah Jr | Dreamstime.com; p11 inset: Corbis/SuperStock; p12 main: © Lee Torrens | Dreamstime.com; p12 inset: © John Leaver | Dreamstime.com; p13 left: JTB Photo/SuperStock; p13 middle: © Ken Cole | Dreamstime.com; p13 right: © Robwilson39 | Dreamstime.com; p14 main: Food and Drink/SuperStock; p14 inset: © Phillip Minnis | Dreamstime.com; p15 left: Fairfax Images/AFR/Andrew Quilty; p15 right: © Fotosearch / SuperStock; p16 main: Getty Images/Stone/Peter Cade; p16 inset: iStockphoto.com/ © kali9; p17: Getty Images; p18 main: © Anne-Louise Quarfoth; p18 inset: iStockphoto.com/ © Wdstock; p19 top: © Viorel Dudau | Dreamstime.com; p19 bottom: © Mathew Hayward | Dreamstime.com; p20 top: Stock Connection/SuperStock; p20 bottom: iStockphoto.com/ © Linda More; p21: iStockphoto.com/ © Juanmonino; p22 top (both); iStockphoto.com/ © kali9; p22 bottom left: iStockphoto.com/ © Hammondovi; p22 bottom right: iStockphoto.com/ © Christina Norwood; p23 top left (and back cover and title page): © Petesaloutos | Dreamstime.com; p23 bottom left: iStockphoto.com/ © Mikhail Kokhanchikov; p23 right: iStockphoto.com/ © Francisco Romero

Contents

City Life

Life in the city can be busy and exciting. The city has tall buildings and crowds of people. There are many cars and buses, and the city roads have traffic lights. The streets are full of shops and offices, as well as banks and large stores.

Very tall buildings are called skyscrapers.

Farm Life

Life on a country farm can be very busy, but it can also be very peaceful. There is plenty of open space with hills and valleys. There are fewer people about and less traffic on the roads than in the city. The farms might have cattle, sheep, pigs or chickens. Other farms grow fruit, vegetables or *grain crops*.

City Houses

Most city people live in houses in the *suburbs*. Suburbs are found away from the centre of the city.

Houses in or near the city are often quite close together. These houses might have a front garden or a back garden, or both. Sometimes people's homes are on top of each other in a *block of flats*. Many people in the city live several *storeys* up.

FAST FACTS

Some flats have a *balcony* so people can sit or stand outside.

Farmhouses

Farmhouses are not normally close to each other — instead they are surrounded by land. Farmhouses can be made of brick or timber. They can be one storey or two storeys high.

FAST FACTS

Sometimes, a *neighbour's* farmhouse might be many miles away.

? What type of house do you live in?

Work in the City

In the city, most people work in offices, banks and shops. Some big shops have hundreds of people working there. The workers stand at the check-out or behind counters, or they walk around and help *customers*.

In summer, lots of people eat their lunch in the city's parks.

People also work in the city *cafés* and *restaurants*. Cooks and chefs *prepare* the food for customers.

Some police officers and firefighters work in the city.

The city also has big hospitals where many doctors and nurses work.

Work on a Farm

Most farm work is done outdoors.

On a cattle farm, dogs may help to bring the cows in for milking or move them into *yards* for *branding*.

On a sheep farm, dogs help to round up the sheep for *shearing*. Farm workers shear the sheep, and the wool is bundled up and sold.

Farmers have to check and fix the fences all around their land. They also have to keep their tractors, *machinery* and other *equipment* running well.

Some farmers grow crops such as tomatoes, strawberries, maize, wheat or apples. Workers on these farms harvest the crops. This means that they cut or gather the crops when they are ready. Other workers help to pack the harvested crops for markets.

If you were helping on a farm, what work might you do?

City Buildings

In the city centre the streets are lined with tall buildings. There are *business* offices, banks and shops. Large stores sell clothing, furniture and other things for the home. Cities also have blocks of flats where people live.

FAST FACTS

Some skyscrapers are so tall they disappear into the clouds.

The city has many cafés and restaurants where people eat. There are also parks with grass, trees and pathways. The *art galleries* and *museums* are good places to visit.

 If you had a whole day to spend in the city, what would you do?

Farm Buildings

Some of the buildings you find on a farm are *barns* and machinery sheds. There might be kennels for working dogs or stables for horses. If the farm has sheep, there will be sheep pens and there might be shearing sheds. Farms with crops have packing sheds or hay sheds.

FAST FACTS

Some shearing sheds are so big that thousands of sheep can be *shorn* in a day.

Normally, farms are not far from country towns. These towns have fewer shops than the city and not many large stores. There will often be a general store where people shop. A general store sells many different things, from washing powder to baby food.

Schools for City Children

Most city schools are large, with hundreds or even thousands of children. These schools have lots of classrooms, hallways and lockers. City schools normally have sports grounds and *gymnasiums*. They might have basketball courts, tennis courts and swimming pools. There might be music rooms and computer rooms, too.

Schools for Farm Children

Most farm children go to small country schools. These have fewer teachers and classrooms than a city school. Sometimes all the children might be in one room, with the younger and older children learning together. A country school will have a sports ground and lots of space to play.

? What is your school like? Do you have lots of space to play?

Getting Around the City

People living in the city often catch a train, bus or tram to work. This is called 'public transport'. Catching public transport means that you travel with lots of other people.

Getting to School

Some city children catch public transport to school. Others go to school by car or bike.

Getting Around a Farm

Farmers often ride motorbikes around their farm, checking fences or looking for sick animals. Sometimes they might drive a car or tractor, or even ride a horse.

FAST FACTS

Some farmers fly over their farm in a helicopter to check that everything is in order.

Getting to School

Farm children often catch a bus to school.
Some are driven to school by their parents,
while others might ride a bike if the school
is not too far away.

? **How do you get to school?**

City Life or Farm Life?

Some children think that living in the city is best because there are lots of fun things to do.

Some children think that living on a farm is best because there are plenty of farm animals and you can even own your own horse.

Which do you think is best — living in the city or living on a farm?

What are the fun things you like to do where you live?

Glossary

art galleries: places where art is displayed

balcony: a platform attached to the outside of a building so that people can sit or stand outside

barns: buildings where animals and the things needed on a farm are kept

block of flats: a building made up of small flats where people live

branding: putting a mark on an animal to show where it comes from

business: to do with work or trade

cafés: snack bars or coffee shops

grain crops: fields of plants grown for their seeds

customers: people who buy things

equipment: tools or items needed for a job

gymnasiums: a large hall for games and exercise

machinery: tools with many parts that help people in their work

museums: places where interesting things are displayed

neighbour: a person who lives nearby

prepare: to get something ready

restaurants: places where people pay to have meals

shearing/shorn: cutting off a sheep's wool

storeys: different levels (floors) of a house or building

suburbs: homes and shops around the centre of a city

yards: small areas with fences

Index